# Signature Play

lyrical poems

## Jane LeCroy

with music by Tom Abbs

THREE ROOMS PRESS

NEW YORK CITY

*Signature Play*



Editor:
Peter Carlaftes

Cover and Interior Design:
KG Design International, New York, NY
www.katgeorges.com

Front cover photos by Kitty Gritt (www.gritt.net), except for photo of 10-year-old Jane by the author's father, Gary Hohenberger, and photo of Jane with mic by Jay Franco (www.venti20vision.com). Drawing of Jane with hair in bun by daughter Alice Luna at age 8. Drawing of Jane with hair down by friend Noor at age 8.

Back cover photo by David Schloss (www.facebook.com/DavidSchlossPhoto).

First Edition
ISBN: 978-0-9884008-7-0

Published by
Three Rooms Press, New York, NY
www.threeroomspress.com

*For Dorian,*

*who changed my signature and shapes my play*

## THERE WAS A LOVE CHILD WENT FORTH 1973

The velvety breath of marijuana forever circling my house
My father's gentle hands loving his guitar
The sweet smoky smell of my mother's black hair
Her bare feet and brown hands
Her womb full of my brother
Then Gary's tiny new hands on my face

The tap of the bottle against the mug
Spilling pink Pepto-Bismol on the oriental living room carpet
My purple tricycle
The dreaming forest echoing the thruway
That tumbled by like ocean waves
Stripping naked in the woods
How white my body was against the earth
The wild strawberries that mysteriously gave me poison ivy
Watching the deer's hot breath as they ate in winter

Papa Hutt, dead, open coffin
Our basement with egg-cartoned walls
The giant sawdust camel and stick horse
The hiss, in winter, of the radiators
Gary and I in the blue fish baby pool,
    underwater he believed my hair was angels
My father disappearing for hours into the basement
The two married trees that stood in the yard
My two married parents
My mother crying

My mom, like a circus performer
    eating marshmallows that were on fire
The huge building blocks at my nursery school
Falling down the yellow and blue twisty slide at King's Park
My kindergarten that was a boiler room
    and smelled like burning dust and manila paper

The brown and yellow flowered kitchen wall paper
Falling down the wooden stairs with Gary because
        we dusted them so clean and slippery
                while Rory was being born

Uncle Eric, 22, shooting himself in the head
Rory getting the red and yellow truck from the top of the coffin
Grandpa canoeing the ashes out with a six-pack
        to scatter and sink in the Hudson
My grandmother's green lumpy rug
        that I could smooth one way and push on to make a picture
Andrew Lynch's red umbrella
Our first kiss near the stove
My mom tying yellow pencils to my overalls, with
        colored ribbons, so that I wouldn't lose them
Watching my brown braids swing in front of my face
                                        on the bus or running
Running
The windy walk to the bus stop

The sound of hate from a man's mouth
The sting of blacktop on the palms of the hands
Trying to collect enough honeysuckle to drink
My Ernie and Bert birthday party blowing away in the wind
The weight of my lunch box with a Thermos
        as opposed to without one
The way cocaine looks on a mirror
        when it's the only thing my father lit in a dark room
It's a dense galaxy made up of tiny stars

contents

I HAVE MY GUN . . . . . . . . . . 1
BULLET . . . . . . . . . . 3
BAD MAP . . . . . . . . . . 4
DRAW ME . . . . . . . . . . 8
TRAVELING . . . . . . . . . . 9
SLINGSHOT . . . . . . . . . . 10
I MADE IT RAIN . . . . . . . . . . 12
BUILD YOUR OWN HOME . . . . . . . . . . 16
NEW YORK CITY . . . . . . . . . . 18
THIS FLOOR . . . . . . . . . . 21
MERMAID SAYS . . . . . . . . . . 24
EPISTLE FOR THE END OF SUMMER . . . . . . . . . . 25
NEPTUNE . . . . . . . . . . 31
AIRBORNE . . . . . . . . . . 33
FLYING PIECE . . . . . . . . . . 35
LOST MY WAY . . . . . . . . . . 36
MENISCUS . . . . . . . . . . 39
MOSQUITO . . . . . . . . . . 40
MOONSCAPE . . . . . . . . . . 42
DARKNESS . . . . . . . . . . 45
SHAPE OF . . . . . . . . . . 47
LITTLE BIT FURTHER AWAY . . . . . . . . . . 48
LAST DANCE . . . . . . . . . . 53
SAVE ME . . . . . . . . . . 54
PRAYING MANTIS . . . . . . . . . . 57
BROKEN HEART . . . . . . . . . . 59
FALLEN CREATURE . . . . . . . . . . 62
SWEAR . . . . . . . . . . 63
SWITCHPLATE . . . . . . . . . . 65
REDEMPTION SONG . . . . . . . . . . 66
BORDERS . . . . . . . . . . 67
NEEDLE WORKER . . . . . . . . . . 76

SHOE REPAIR .... 77
ALICE SAVINO .... 79
THUNDERBOLT .... 82
RHINOCEROS .... 84
A STORY WITH ICEBERGS .... 86
BIG BLACK HABIT .... 95
WONDERELLA MARVELLA .... 97
LINER NOTES .... 101
ABOUT THE AUTHOR AND COMPOSER .... 106

ignature
lay

## I HAVE MY GUN

I have my gun
I have my fire
There is no God
I have my choir
I have my time
I have my might
The sun is lie
It's just a tiny light
In the black black sky
Eternal night

The stars all go out
Their light a trick
They all burn down
The darkness is thick
Everything tries
Everything fails
This life is a cross
And a bunch of nails

I'm gonna open
I'm gonna cry
My tears a flood
Float me to die
Is defeat survival?
Is death a life?
The answer is yes
There is no best
It is the least
We are all beasts

Look at our teeth
Look at us howl
Look at us laugh
Look at us growl

I'm on fire
I'm a light
I'm going out
I have my might
I have my gun
I have my fire
I am a star
I have my choir
The sun is a liar
The sun is a lie
It's just a tiny light
In the black black sky
Eternal night

## BULLET

Thrown into the heat, the fire drink me down
been looking for you but you're not around

Our bodies were loaned to us, I don't know by who
but if you don't take care of yourself, no one's gonna take care of you

We litter in our streets, we contaminate the land
then we wonder why we sleep in garbage and eat poison

You are the bullet in your head
I don't have to kill you
because you're the assassin that'll make sure you're dead

Life is a funeral procession where we're chasing each other around
we fight to live in boxes then we end up in one underground

I'm tired of planting flowers you'll only kill them for me when I'm sick
the Earth needs them more than me; if I plant them again they'll say,
*DO NOT PICK*!

We send pictures through the air, the rich are on the internet
money gets more technology and the poor go deeper in debt

Look and see where schools have computers
Look and see where the schools are with none
Look at the ratio of black men in college compared to prison

The TV says, *It tastes fine!* So we drink up our oppression
to get some more we wait on line and take drugs for the depression

We're at both ends of the barrel and we're all too trigger happy
the top of the food chain has no predators so we're our own worst enemy

One little piggy went to market, one little piggy stayed home
one little piggy ate roast beef, one little piggy packed a gun
one little piggy shot all the others and now there are none

## BAD MAP

*based on Edgar Allan Poe's "Eldorado"*

My big heart broke
it broke down,
down the long road
where I was.
I want to go back
but I got a bad map,
I feel wrong
and I'm right,
I can't find
my Eldorado.

You want to go back
but you can't,
you got a bad map
like your hand,
scarred up so fine
can't read the lines
worn down by time
now you can't find
your Eldorado.

If you ask the Shadow
the Shade replies,
ride, boldly ride
ride, boldly ride
over the Mountains
of the Moon,
down the Valley
of the Shadow.
Seek Eldorado.

# Bad Map

♩ = 82
Jane LeCroy and Tom Abbs
Voice
Violoncello
Vc.
2
4
6
My big heart broke it broke down, down the long road where I was. I want to go back but I got a bad map I feel wrong and I'm
You want to go back but you can't, you got a bad map like your hand, scarred up so fine can't read the lines worn down by time now you can't
If you ask the Shadow the shade re - plies, ride bold - ly ride ride boldly ride o - ver the Mountains of the Moon, down the Vall - ey of the Shad -

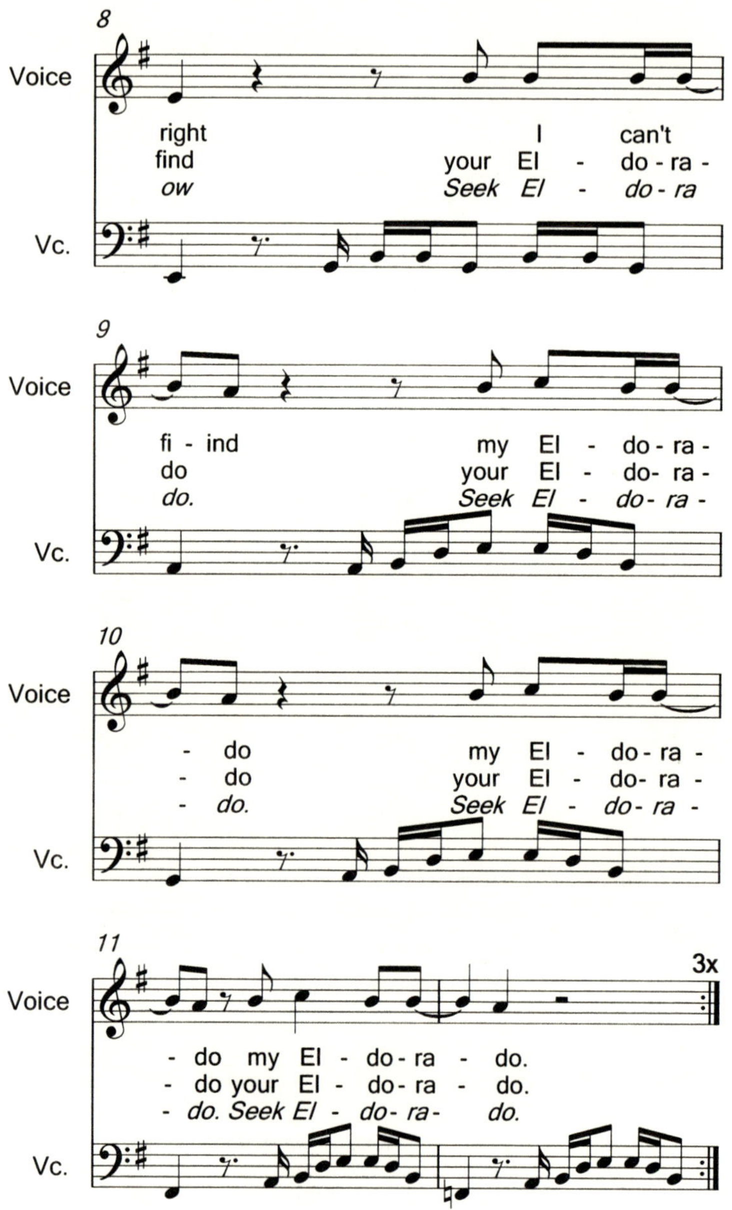
8
Voice
right I can't
find your El - do - ra -
ow Seek El - do - ra
Vc.
9
Voice
fi - ind my El - do - ra -
do your El - do- ra -
do. Seek El - do- ra -
Vc.
10
Voice
- do my El - do - ra -
- do your El - do- ra -
- do. Seek El - do- ra -
Vc.
11
Voice
3x
- do my El - do - ra - do.
- do your El - do - ra - do.
- do. Seek El - do- ra- do.
Vc.

13
Ad lib ad nauseum al fine
Voice
Vc.
15
Voice
Vc.
16
Voice
Vc.
Fine

## DRAW ME

I miss you, I love you, I want you to stay
my heart is on fire, I'm melting away
I want you, I have you, everything is fine
I'm lying, I'm tired, I wish you were mine

Draw me in, I'm drawn
Draw on me
Draw me

I try to keep my dreams inside my head
but my recurring nightmare shows me my death
I'm living, I'm dying, my heart messed with my head
I want you, I have you, my passion, my dread

The only thing saving me is all the art
I stare as you make it, I feel I'm a part
a part of the paper, your hands and your mind
the texture reveals me in curves that you find

Come here now land in me
you know you love when we play
I'm singing, I'm startled, I smile anyway
I miss you, I love you, I want you to stay
my heart is on fire, I'm melting away

## TRAVELING

I know to follow the black river home
With moon in my eyes, the light for the dream
At night one must always travel alone

The road I journey is one that has grown
In my head during dark, crazed like a fiend
I know to follow the black river home

Walking the long bridge, its metal, its bone
I hear myself rhythm the road at its seam
At night one must always travel alone

But it's always for you that I end why I roam
My motion is narrow, no in-between
I know to follow the black river home

You're in my voice when I hear myself moan
You pull me to where you are with your scream
At night one must always travel alone

Although at the end of each track I've sewn
You've been the light, what leads is the stream
I know to follow the black river home
At night one must always travel alone

## SLINGSHOT

Are you crazy about yourself?
It's easy to see when you walk down the street
that you think you're the beauty. . . . beauty
I'm gonna kill you, I'm gonna rip your heart out with a spoon
and don't think that I love you because I never did

You like my pupils black and wide
because you have another intention
when you look deep into my eyes
you seek your own reflection
because you're conceited

It's so nice to eat when you have to eat
It's so nice to pee when you have to pee
It's so nice to love when you have to

But I don't want to, don't have to, not going to

You think you're so smart and so sexy
you think I'll wait for you a long time
well, I got a big love that's distractible
it won't wait for you to be mine

My love is a slingshot, not a boomerang
I ride once and not again
I do the damage
use the door
I'm ok by myself

Don't like: *mirror-mirror on the wall*
*mirror-mirror on the wall*
not me, not me, not me

## I MADE IT RAIN

I made it rain, I made a rainbow
in the driveway I used a garden hose
Sometimes I'm God, this life is Heaven
Sometimes it's Hell, when I'm the Devil

Don't believe in the Bible's Jesus
not Mohammed or Torah's Moses
no religion, monotheism
I be hatin' on all their judgin'

Some people think that there are reasons
for everything in life that happens
but it's our power to find the magic
in everything that is tragic

That is tragic

Don't blame God or the Devil,
no absolute Good or Evil
We make up meaning, human being

Human being

# I Made It Rain

Jane LeCroy and Tom Abbs

10
Voice
Don't be - lieve
Some peo - ple
Don't blame
Vc.
12
Voice
in, the Bi - ble's Je - sus not Mo
think that there are reas ons for ev - ery
God or the dev - il no ab - so-
Vc.
14
Voice
hamm-ed or To-rah's Mo - ses no rel
thing in life that happ-ens but it's our
lute good or ev - il We make up
Vc.
16
Voice
i - gion Mo - no the - ism I be
pow - er to find the mag - ic in ev - ery
mean-ing, hu-man be - ing ...
Vc.

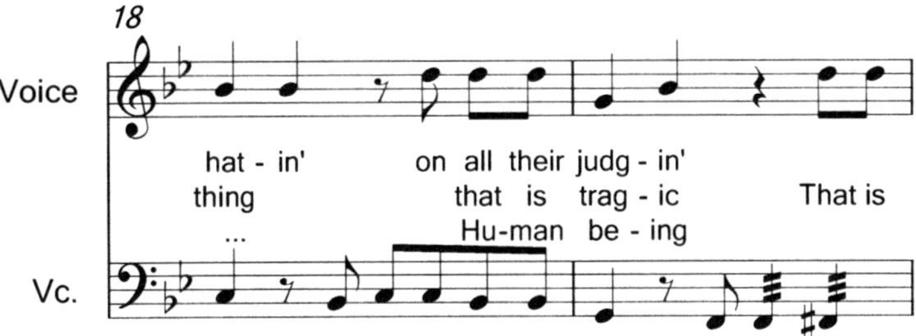
18
Voice
hat - in' on all their judg - in'
thing that is trag - ic That is
... Hu-man be - ing
Vc.

20
Voice
...
trag - ic
...
Vc.

22
4x
Voice
I made it
Vc.

23
Repeat ad lib al fine
Voice
(straight)
Fine
Vc.

## BUILD YOUR OWN HOME

*It's a world for the beautiful, the ugly have no home*

Manny built his house in the desert out of tires
 he eats cactus soup and likes his lizards on toast.
Ani built a tree house in the Redwoods out of scrap wood
 the rain coming down sounds like a thousand tin roofs.
Susan built her house on the beach made out of driftwood
 pulled from shipwrecks, flotsam, jetsam.
Danny made his house out of an abandoned railroad tunnel
 he sings himself to sleep and his voice is amplified.

Make your own clothes
Build your own house
Love your own body
Live your own dream

Laws are about money, not me or you
 why should we do what they tell us to?
Everything they plan is such a bloody scandal
 always trying to take our hands from the handle
 by cutting things up to silence our voices
 disguised as convenience they take our choices.
A brainless nation is for what they are aiming
 when we buy we comply with the system they're making
 by contributing economically to the thing we should be breaking.

They tell you you're a sinner, you're a winner, you're a beginner;
 their judgment wouldn't matter if you believed in yourself.
It's really getting to be such a scary place
 everywhere the news is O.J. Simpson's face.
What are they hiding behind this boring trial?
Surely the nation is in extreme denial.

Cut taxes for pocket change to go to the greedy
    fuck healthcare, education and housing for the needy.
We're all needy, we're all greedy, needy greedy, greedy greedy
But we keep our eyes on the lies because it's easier
    than making a change in the sleaze that's getting sleazier.

You are guilty
I am guilty
We're all guilty, guilty, guilty

## NEW YORK CITY

Sometimes undone the icing has me
she is a lovely New York City
with river limbs dangling sparkling bangles of bridges
The ocean grabs her feet, her edges are beaches

I wish I didn't want her

Her luminous starless nights
glowing skyline, oscilloscope reading of life
her staring holy moon
her extremes of temperature
burning, freezing, lovely
I want to be her thermometer
She leaves me begging, always wanting
always having, always imagining more
I am in awe of her, I need a rest from her
I long for her, long New York City

A bicycle licks her in less than a day
but the life of an eye cannot know her entirety, entirely
her incessant construction, destruction
traffic pulse, ribbons of lanes
veins of underground trains
teeming with dreams, garbage and smells
covered with sores, wounds, riches and bells
wildlife, wild life, we claim to know her well
Giant concrete wishing well

8 million strange strangers each have their own vision
beyond truth, beyond fiction, temptation, religion
impressing the life of each body she touches
she's a movie star, an icon, a history, a country
expensive, compelling, free, sneaky and yelling
gorgeous and lovely, keep secrets and tell me
she is my home my mysterious dwelling
in her I drown and emerge
and keep sailing

I wish I didn't want her

# New York City

Jane LeCroy and Tom Abbs

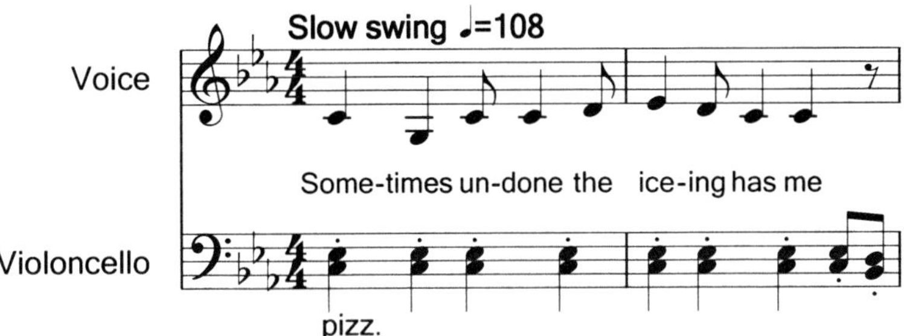

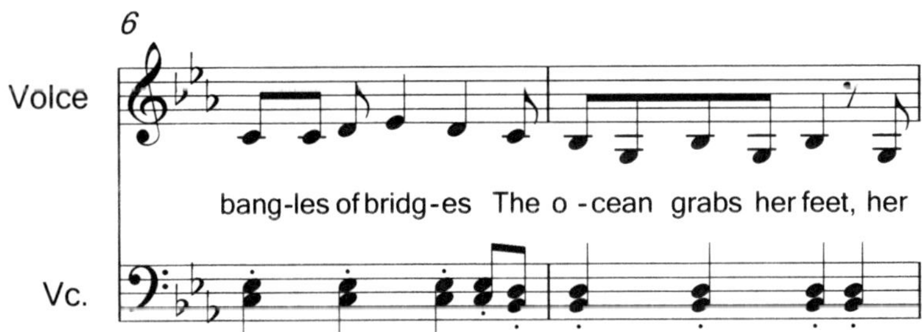

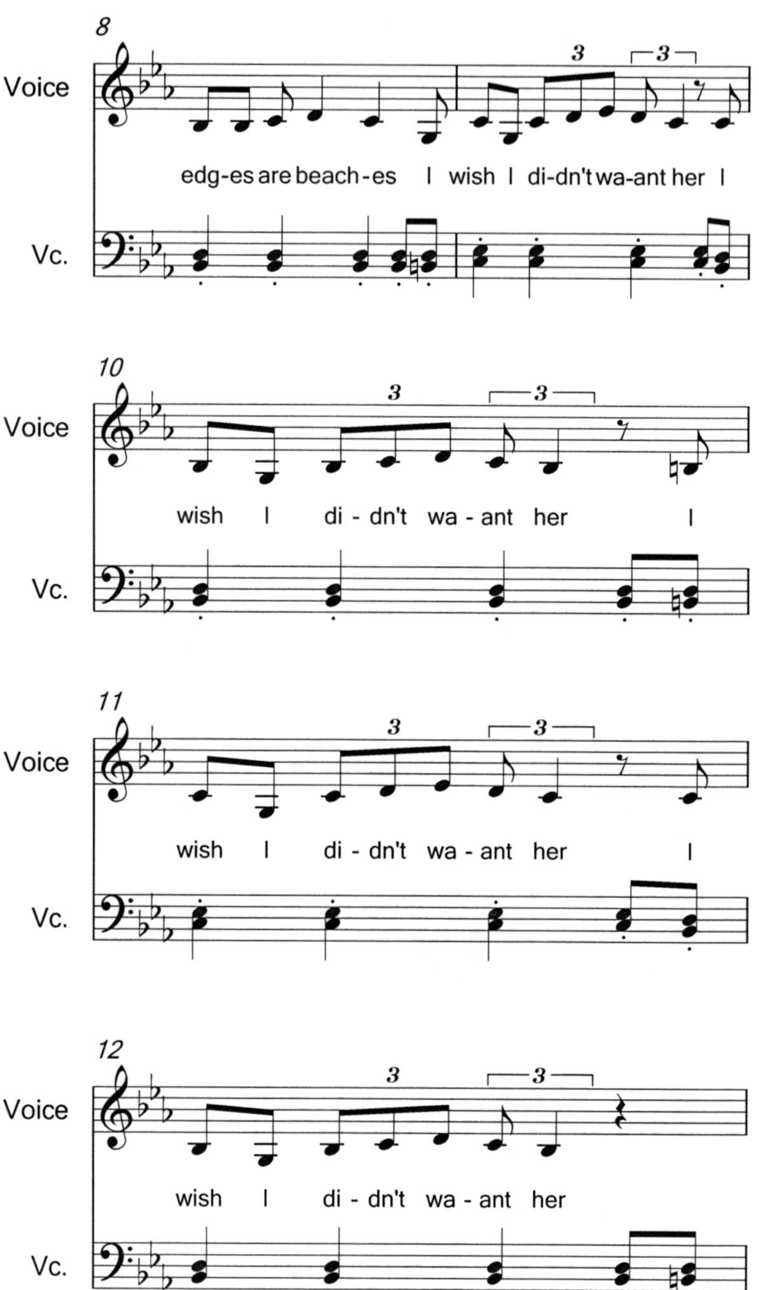
8
Voice
edg-es are beach-es I wish I di-dn't wa-ant her I
Vc.
10
Voice
wish I di - dn't wa - ant her I
Vc.
11
Voice
wish I di - dn't wa - ant her I
Vc.
12
Voice
wish I di - dn't wa - ant her
Vc.

## THIS FLOOR

So stoned
left myself
in the cold
trying to
remember
my lies
talk myself
out of
digging my grave face.
The lines
by my eyes
are a map
to my hole in my soul
in the ground
I'm buried down.
I didn't plan on getting here
I'm just as surprised as you
to be in this warm war
so full of pretty stuff.
I was tricked
into liking computers
the rude nature
of phones and beepers
I hate all this
don't keep in touch.
Phone tag
Beep code
Dial tone
No one home
*Leave a message!*
I want to live out of
this big toy city.
All the people stacked up
with their dishes and clocks.

My bed is heaven but no one wants to stay
too close to death, that's why I'm lonely.
You said it yourself, I'm evil, passing out pleasure
keeping it, giving it. . .
Being mean
Laugh
Whip smart
My knees
still wrinkled from
sucking dick in the shower.
Falling asleep
covered in your cum
it's so peaceful with you
I let go so many of my
metal metaphors
holding me together.

You see me
I am flesh
a tired girl
wanting to hold
your broken self
in the night
smell your smoke skin
the nightmare acid
salt of your sweat
near the truth
the roof of my mouth
my cavities
growing in your cold room
your face story unraveling
making me understand a little
each time you tell me, I want you more.
Beautiful in a true way
your face faded because
all I can see is your heart.
The ocean floor sports another reality,
sharks flinging seals up into their jaws.
You always make me late
and I don't mind.

## MERMAID SAYS

mythic chic, think, wink
find her at your bathroom sink
scratched, scathed and scraped
no easy escape
no superhero cape
to drape around the nape

fill me in, I'm a blank, fill me in

sexy complexi
life in full flexi
ocean is no sin
a potion is any opening
I like when you text me
but better when you're next to me

no cheater believer
hotter than a heater
you know you want to meet her
greet her, sweet her
sail my mind, sea you'll find
as ice only, water binds

sheltered, pelted
we're all melted
rivuletted and gilded
moon spilled and willed it
I am her, I am here
fleet of tall ships ride and veer
in the river of my ear

can't clear it or steer it
just want to be near it
see bowsprit bow-spirit
if it's truly great we fear it

## EPISTLE FOR THE END OF SUMMER

Dear Lifeguard,
I admit
I have a favorite
You are it

Sitting high all day
up in your white wood throne
Looking out across
the vast ocean
Your surfboard chariot
over the waves
The right directions
your arms wave
To the people
they love you so
you're king of the beach
everyone knows

You're king of the beach
Everyone knows

You don't know this but at night
I climb in your chair and
I watch the moon rise
like a pumpkin
into the sky
to this chair where
you're all soaked in
and it's touching
my bare skin
though no one knows it
I am queen

Though no one knows it
I am queen

# Epistle For The End Of Summer

Jane LeCroy and Tom Abbs

9
Voice
high all day up in your
know this
Vc.
10
Voice
white wood throne look - ing
but at night I climb in your
Vc.

11
Voice
out acr - oss the vast o -
chair and I watch the moon
Vc.

12
Voice
- cean Your surf board
rise Like a
Vc.

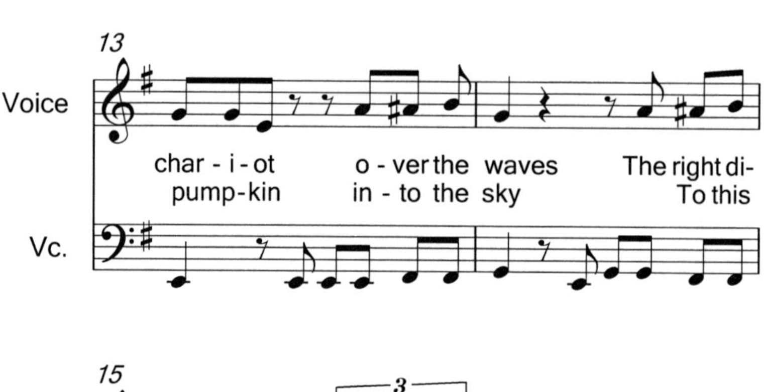
13
Voice
char - i - ot o - ver the waves The right di-
pump-kin in - to the sky To this
Vc.

15
Voice
3
rec - tions your arms wave To the
chair where you're all soaked in And it's
Vc.

17
Voice
peo - ple, they love you so You're
touch-ing my bare skin
Vc.

19
Voice
1. 3
5
king of the beach Ev - ry one kno-ows You're
Vc.

21
Voice
king of the beach
Ev - ry one kno - ows You're
Vc.
23
Voice
king of the beach
Ev - ry one kno - ows
Vc.
25
2.
Voice
Though no one knows it
I am queen
Vc.
27
Voice
Though no one knows it
I am queen
Vc.
29
Voice
Though no one knows it
I am
Vc.

31
Voice
1st time only
queen.
(Free-verse ad lib al fine)
Vc.
33
Vc.
35
Vc.
37
Vc.
39
Vc.
41
Vc.
43
Fine
Vc.

## NEPTUNE

I'm dreaming about Neptune
I'm dreaming about the king of the sea because I want to see
    and I want to sail away home

Am I any better off, than how I was before?
No matter what I had, I was always wanting more
So, I'm always at the beginning
It's always my first step
Anywhere I ever was, was somewhere I left

Neptune, Neptune
I'm requesting a ticket, I'm ready to ride
    the back of a whale to find Atlantis again
Neptune, I want to make a trade
    turn my legs in to be a mermaid
I want my skin, to change to scales
I want my bones to make a fish tail

I'm from Atlantis!
I'm so blue I'm sure I belong to you,
Neptune

If you take me underwater
I'll be your daughter
I'll shine your crown if you take me down
I go to Coney Island, to try and find my way
I hear the Cyclone screaming
    as the waves climb on the beach

The salty hands don't take me
They don't take me
I ask a single seagull
        to tell the secret of the sea
She dove and got a fish and left me

I only want one thing
        and that is to be free
I can't do it breathing this air so

                drown me

I don't want to want anymore!
Atlantis free me from desire!

                Drown me

## AIRBORNE

You were airborne
  like a running dog who knows how to fly

When you stopped I came so hard, I thought I was airborne

And the sign said –
I read it:
  Please don't smoke, Don't litter, No radio
  Free ear piercing with repair of torn earlobe
  Pull for emergency stop

And I'm on the train
in transit

When the train came in so hard, I thought it was airborne

And the sky is a promise of eternal distance
we will never be any closer than this
the tracks cross but the trains don't
they only pass and glide by
Bye bye

## FLYING PIECE

Sometimes I wish I were dead
my body floating out over the sea
Perfection finally reached through non-existence
Perfection finally reached without me

Sometimes I wish I were free
but freedom you make
you can't give or take
Perfection doesn't reach reality

Once I was just a flying piece of love inside my mother's life
        the touchless touch of infinity caressing me eternally
I live here

The seagulls are laughing
the seagulls are picking through the garbage
I lost my first name on the way home from Coney Island
the seagulls are flying away

Sometimes I wish I were wrong
but the days stretch forever long
I sing off my wings, I float and I ring
I land but I don't know the song

Sometimes I wish I were sure
but certainty we fake
to wait is to mistake
a door is any hole in the wall

The people are laughing
the people are picking through the garbage
I lost all expectations on my way home from Coney Island
the people are flying away

Once I was just a flying piece of love inside my mother's life
        the touchless touch of infinity caressing me eternally
I live here

*Scan the above QR code to access*
*the musical rendition of this piece*
*performed by*
*Jane LeCroy (vocals) and Tom Abbs (electric bass & cello).*

## LOST MY WAY

I have gone and lost my way
I don't think I'll ever stay
anywhere for very long
something's always going wrong

I fear I might disappear
I fear I am not here
the sky can't hold me
the moon, it tries
pulls the water out my eyes

The eyes are brain exposed
like the tongue is muscle
and the teeth are bones
the face is the place you can look and see
into the depths of biology

I got a lock but not a key
the lock I got is me

Look at all the people
I am one of them
walking their sorrow
their loss, their joy, their sin

The one I love is not mine
but then no one ever is
no one ever is
0
1 2 3 4 5 6 7 8 9
Numbers go on forever
but that is all of them
quantified, quantified

I am lone and lonely
no one's sadness can compare to me
but look at all the people
crying, crying
each one is sure
of the depths of their own misery
misery, misery quantified
and I am one of them
I am one of them
I have gone and lost my way

*Scan the above QR code to access*
*the musical rendition of this piece*
*performed by*
*Jane LeCroy (vocals) and Tom Abbs (electric bass).*

## MENISCUS

I just got here
and already you want me to leave
Leave

I turned into a dolphin to swim across the ocean
I turned into a magpie to fly across the sky
I turned into a man to walk across the bad land
I turned into a mole to dig a hole underground

I climbed up this mountain top to see if I could see you
could not see you, climbed back down

I turned into a water bug to walk across the lake skin
thinking that my stick-star shape would get you to let me in
I learned to walk the meniscus just to get a kiss
Kiss

What I want to give is not what you want to receive
have mercy on me, Possessiveness
have mercy on me, Long Term Desire

I love the Leos, the Leos don't love me
I chase the lions and the lions kill me

My life isn't anything
compared to stars or sound,
sound,
sound,
sound

## MOSQUITO

I hear crickets
the sky is growing dark
and tiny things are taking my blood

I'd talk about the moon
but that's what I always do
here I go again, its light is through me

A planet appears
steady is its light
it comes to my eyes, on the edge of this night

I've tried to trust people
the way I trust rocks and fire in the sky
but never were my eyes left dry

Most of the world is hidden
in places where language can't reach
but I've been searching for the right words
to describe every and each
and I'll never ever ever ever ever find them
because they don't exist

These words are rockets that will never land
because your planet doesn't understand
my specific gravity
you are unable to capture me
as if I'm a wavelength you cannot see
no matter how hard I transmit you won't receive me
Receive me, receive me

Maybe I still love you
I envy mosquitoes
they land on you and take your blood

Most of love is hidden
in places where language can't reach
but I've been searching for the right words
to define every and each
and I'll never ever ever ever ever have you
because we don't exist

No matter how I transmit, you won't receive me
despite how clear I want to be,
the signals I send are just noisy, noisy
like insects loud in the night
their song is undecipherable, it is undecipherable
like the dark side of the moon from here
and the song of insects

Mosquito

*Scan the above QR code to access*
*the musical rendition of this piece*
*performed by*
*Jane LeCroy (vocals) and Tom Abbs (electric bass).*

## MOONSCAPE

You reveal yourself to me

The moon comes out a piece at a time
the heavens reveal their motions sublime
the stars appear to move but they stay still
I hope such deception is not your desire and will

Even though the moon's surface is dry
the craters are named as bodies of water, wishful lies
it's fantasy, we try, humanity dreams
and from this we fall and we fly

We landed originally on the Sea of Tranquility
but the Sea of Moisture leads to the Sea of Clouds
then there's the Ocean of Storms
as if the Sea of Crisis is where we were bound

Sometimes this life can feel like the Marsh of Decay
with the Sea of Cold and the Lake of Death
but we must remember, there are other places and names
the Bay of Rainbows is next to the Sea of Rains

I focus on the Sea of Serenity deep
as I walk with you across the Marsh of Sleep
I'd like to live with you in the Lake of Dreams
but the moon is black & white and we are colorful beings

If space is expanding and everything is moving further apart
the further things get, the more room I may have in my heart
I may get the patience to deliver me higher
but I don't want to be a rock covered with other's desires,
    like the moon
No, I don't want to be a rock covered with others' desires

Please, reveal yourself to me

*Scan the above QR code to access*
*the musical rendition of this piece*
*performed by*
*Jane LeCroy (vocals) and Tom Abbs (acoustic bass).*

## DARKNESS

There is a darkness creeping in
I've seen the world go blank
There are greater mysteries
Than the things I thank
Like the storm on Jupiter
Where we did first meet
Of all the forces in nature
You must love gravity

I am far as all the stars
You held me in your eyes
I reflected there
Like all the fireflies
In night fields of July
The heat pushed on our skin
And our love wore us thin
Our love wore us thin

There is a darkness creeping in
I've seen the world go blank
I've seen myself as an outline and had to fill it in
Delicately, I slipped you into me
When I was feeling empty
You are more camouflage than chameleon skin
You are more slippery than the things with fins
I let you into me, more because I couldn't help it
I didn't write an invitation but there you did move in

Now I'm wondering, wandering
Without the me I used to be –
Does it matter anyway?
Another lost memory –
What are selves anyway?

We're all forgotten after all
Even Fame is a lie, you see
Remembered image is all fiction
          Every moment ghostly

You haunt me now!

And at least leave the lights off so I can glow
Please, at least leave the lights off so I can glow
The moon glides like it used to, but not me, oh not me
Glamorous things used to touch me
Glistening was my skin but I have no matter now
So all the material passes through, ever since you alone, you alone
I alone away from me but thankful to be free of myself

I have no emotion now, no desire, no regret
No longing, no love, no sadness nor hate, no porthole or gate
To let me in, let me in, let me in
Only words connect me to this place
When I stop this I will dissipate

Goodbye, goodbye, goodbye

## SHAPE OF

I know the shapes of
the things that are missing

I lost my song and I want your help
to find the words that I am missing
and your kisses shape the meaning

What does it mean?

I lost my way and I want your help
to find the map that I am missing
and your kisses shape the route

What should I do?

I lost my love and I want your help
to find the heart that I am missing
and your kisses shape the memory

Will you remember me?

I lost my mind and I want your help
to find the dreams that I've been dreaming
and your kisses shape the meaning

What does it mean?

I know the shapes of
the things that are missing

## LITTLE BIT FURTHER AWAY

Just a little bit further away I love you
I love you

Where are we going
        and where have we been
It all looks familiar
        but I'll look at it again
The edges are blurring
        I stared for too long
Eyes are deceivers
        so our ears hear these songs

A tree in the distance
        stays small
In a painting you can't get
        any closer at all
I treasure your letters
        I read them all night
The things that write you
        make me feel all right

The darkness is similar
        to light
Both of them illuminate
        just opposite sides
The light shows the truth
        for the eyes
While the darkness reveals
        what the heart can realize

The dark for the mind
        and the light for the brain
We explain away our losses
        while we justify our gains
It could have been different
        but I like how it is
No matter how we have it
        it's a beautiful kiss

Jane LeCroy and Tom Abbs

**Churning** ♩. = 63

Voice
Just a li-ttle bit furth-er a-way I love

Violoncello
pizz.

2
Voice
you I love you Just a

Vc.

3
Voice
li - ttle bit furth - er a - way I love

Vc.

4
**Last time - To Coda**
Voice
you I love you
A
The
The

Vc.

5

Voice

Where are we go - ing and where have we been? It
tree in the dist ance stay small In a
dark-ness is simil - ar to light
dark for the mind and the light for the brain We ex

Vc.

6

Voice

all looks fam - il - ier but I'll look at it a - gain The
paint-ing you can't get a - ny clo - ser at all I
Both of them ill umin ate just op po site sides The
plain away our loss-es while we justi - fy our gains It

Vc.

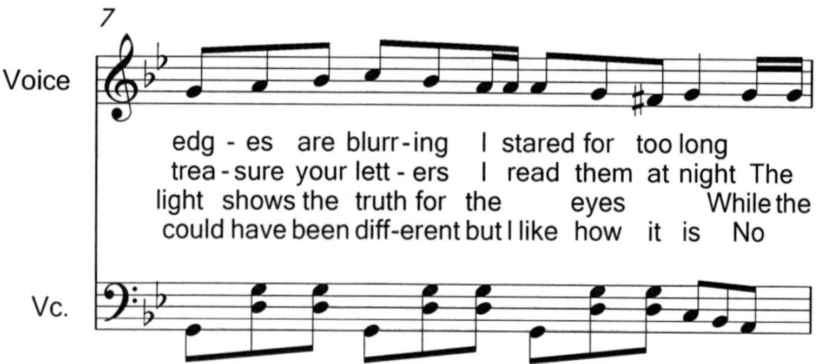

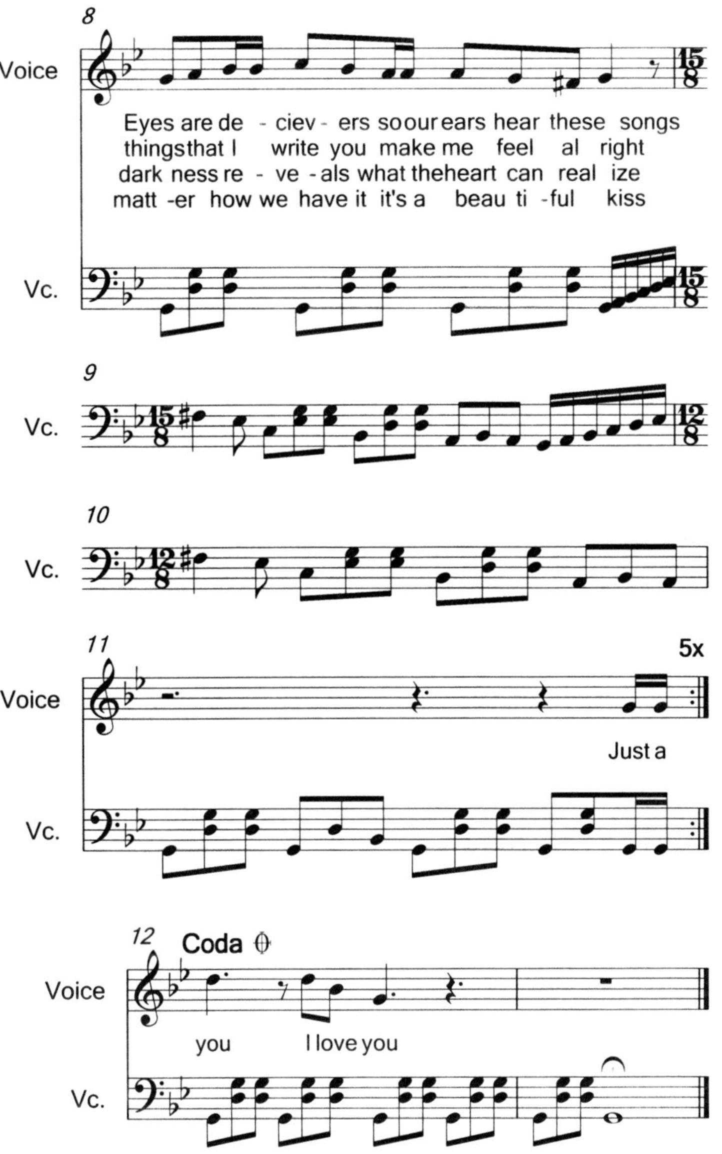
8
Voice
Eyes are de - ciev - ers so our ears hear these songs
things that I write you make me feel al right
dark ness re - ve - als what the heart can real ize
matt -er how we have it it's a beau ti -ful kiss
Vc.
9
Vc.
10
Vc.
11
5x
Voice
Just a
Vc.
12
Coda
Voice
you I love you
Vc.

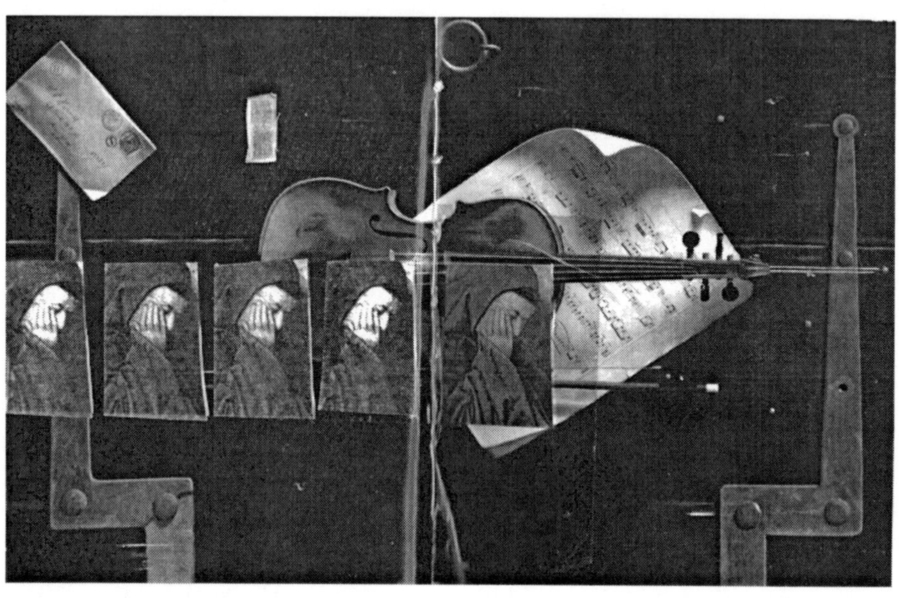

## LAST DANCE

I had the last dance
      the very last dance with you
and I lost my mind
and I lost my mind over you

I remember the temperature
of that room
on my dress

I remember the temperature
of that room
under my dress

I remember the temperature
of your cheek
on my lips

And now every step
      from here to forever
            is a step in that dance
because the very last dance, lasts forever

I remember the last dance
because I'm dancing it still
and it takes my love
and it takes my love, and it takes my will

## SAVE ME

No one can take you from you
or bring you to yourself
you are a stranger it takes your life to meet
there's not bottom to this well

I'm just a girl with open eyes
I don't need to be saved
you are a hungry lifesaver
whose ship is like a grave

You didn't save me
You couldn't save me
Save me, save me
Save me

You're a magnificent castle
a thousand years old
I was seduced by your solitude
now I'm dying of the cold

You're a mirage in the desert
a welcome sight until
you approach the wish that's formed in heat
and there's nothing there to spill

You're like water on the moon
we're not quite sure it's there
though there's lovely evidence that it may exist
the theory is just that

You are a ghost with details
but there's not a story that you tell
I fill the blank that you are with my fear
and you become my greatest thrill

# Save Me

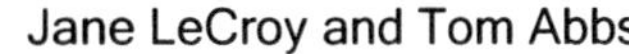
Jane LeCroy and Tom Abbs

Con moto ♩ = 126
Voice
5
No one can take you from you or
Violoncello
pizz.

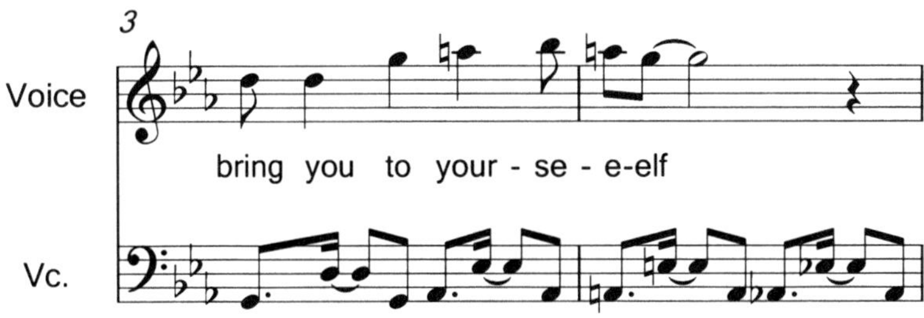
3
Voice
bring you to your - se - e-elf
Vc.

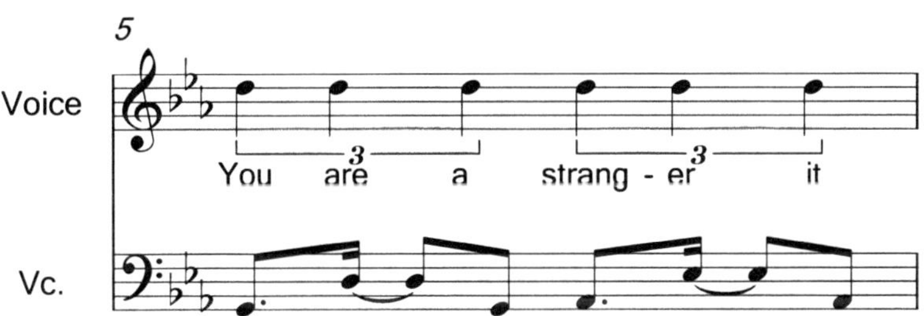
5
Voice
3
3
You are a strang - er it
Vc.

6
Voice
takes your life to meet, There's no
Vc.

7
Voice
bott -om to this well
Vc.
9
Vc.
11
Vc.
13
Voice
I'm just a girl with
Vc.
15
Voice
op-en eyes I don't need to be saved...
Vc.

## PRAYING MANTIS

She'll take me just to break me
she's a praying mantis
moving through the wilderness
and I'm wild wild wild
I want to be her child
I approach her from the back to give her a kiss
Give her a kiss

Oh, I want her, oh so badly
I have loved her, moonly, madly
she lets me come give her my love
just to kill me

I've loved her since the leaves
came from nothing onto branches
the forest is her mansion
my life is for her ransom

Her head is like a flower
I want her every hour
I see her by the water
Summer's only daughter

Only birds have caught her
but her giant eyes
invite me to try
her green wings they start to sing . . .

she's so lovely, lovely, lovely
she's so lovely, lovely ugly
she's so lovely, mean mean lady
she so lovely, so so lovely
lovely, ugly

slow slow moving
now my head's crushed
in her jaws my blood like gravy
in her claws, sticky sticky
she's not picky, spiny spiny
her legs grasp me
It's too late!

and she's so lovely, lovely ugly
mean mean lady, she's so sorry
so so sorry, she's so sorry...

Right?!

## BROKEN HEART

Oh my broken heart is broken
I have another part of my body
That is bigger than my bone, heart, mind, soul, life
Life
It is bigger than parts you know from songs
Parts that work amazing with adrenaline
It is greater than parts that are metaphors for love or pain
More complex than anatomy book dreams
It is another part, it has no name
To explain
And it is breaking
It is breaking
And it is King
It is King

# Broken Heart

Jane LeCroy and Tom Abbs

9
Voice
Vc.
It is bigg-er than parts you know from
Parts that work a - maz - ing with a -
11
Voice
Vc.
songs
dren-a-line
13
Voice
Vc.
It is great-er thanparts that are met-a-phors
15
Voice
Vc.
for love or pain

## FALLEN CREATURE

I am a fallen creature
who knows my way
around the ground

I know insects
worms and arachnids
I know silken threads
the stickiness of woven webs

I speak to xylem and phloem
I know where roots come tendril home
I speak to burrowing dwellers
and get the tour of many cellars

I made a promise long ago
I gave up the sky to live below
my heart was heavy at that time
now it's gone and I'm not mine

The price of love is never cheap
but the price of not loving is eternal sleep
the ink of the promise is dripping still
Whoever said we have free will?

I've been waiting for the ink to dry
and I don't think it will,
ever

Nothing quite lays
like the moon on the water,
a thousand bright pieces
left from the sun's slaughter
and I wish I could follow you

I wish I could follow you

## SWEAR

You held me in your broken arms
kissed my broken skin
I ran my broken tongue along
all your broken teeth
All promises are broken
Love: an armed, masked thief

We kissed and pressed and touched and sighed
until we felt the grief
The breaks they ached of our mistakes
and sang our ballads sweet and sad
How can this beauty that frees relief
be considered bad?

We hold each other in this broken army
we fight the war against Time
No one ever really gets another
but I swear you feel like mine
No one ever really gets another
but I swear you feel like mine

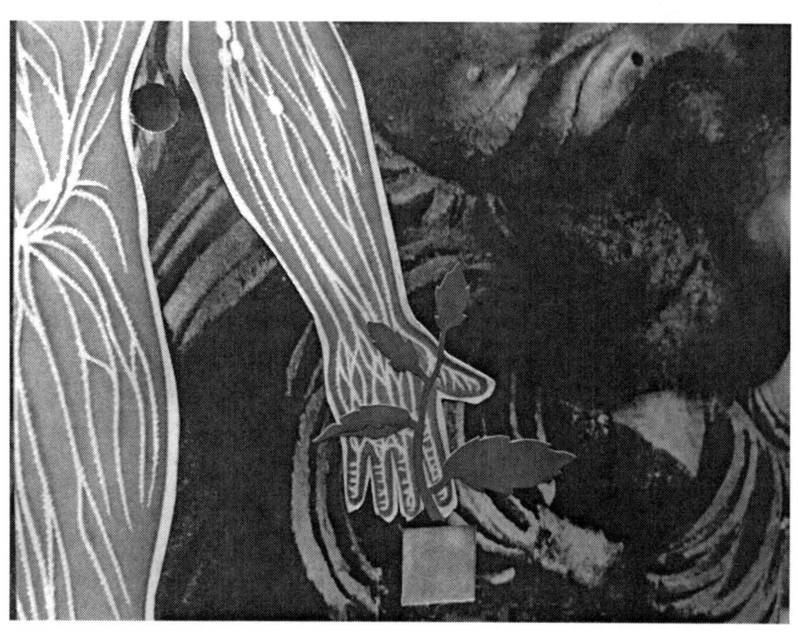

## SWITCHPLATE

Your blue veins have me tied down
Your center is always the middle of your eye black
Your skin is covering you, perfect shining
To look at you with my hands the way I want to would take years

Each moment of you folds eternity
You are made of galaxies
Your humid breath is nebulae becoming stars
Gazing at you makes me an astronomer

Our bodies folding, material doubled over
bending back, overlap,
narrowing, tightening, widening,
wrapper backing, binding, tying

We are a circuit when I am in
the outer space of you
Time traveling electricity
Chaos is the ghost that narrates this story

On a rainy day I get vertigo
looking into a puddle reflecting the sky,
infinity in an inch
Infinity

Reflections do not stick
to the surfaces that show them,
if they did, my tears would leak
a puzzle of your face

We are supernatural, extraterrestrial,
serpentine, turning, winding, spiraling, arching, spanning,
stretching, hooking, coil, ravel, unravel,
repeat, open, close

## REDEMPTION SONG

Even the garbage is better off than me
it is recyclable, organized neatly
it is wrapped tight, I am not

On Wednesday someone will come to pick it up in a truck
I could sit here my whole life and no one would give a fuck

Been falling out of love so I got lots of time
where once my love was, the universe fills my mind
it makes me so lonely I need a rocket ship
just to move faster through the loneliness

Wish I were a tin can then someone could redeem me

Maybe I'd get recycled in to a rocket ship
then I'd move faster through all of it
because all the stars bring so much space, it's falling me apart
been looking through my broken body, cannot find my heart

Mars is the planet of broken hearts
that's why it's red, from the blood of that part
I am so blue you may think I'm from Earth
but if you look inside me, you'll see it's much worse

Garbage already covers the face of the moon
Wish I were a tin can, I'd get there real soon

Because even the garbage is better off than me

## BORDERS

Bodies of water scattered through the park
I walk the walk in the light and the dark
I wait for a monster to jump out at me
With these expectations I'm even scared of the trees
The branches reach up and scrape the breeze
The roots reach down and use capillary action
In the city, action in the city

I don't want to carry identification anymore
I don't want to prove I was born in 1973
I don't want to belong to a country anymore
I don't want to carry photo ID

Bodies of water have edges
Lakes and streams and what's in between
Fields and plains and mountain ranges
Highlands and lowlands and badlands
have edges

And our hands try to make more
We draw lines on the planet with law – WAR!
I don't want to obey anymore
No, I don't want to obey anymore

# Borders

Jane LeCroy and Tom Abbs

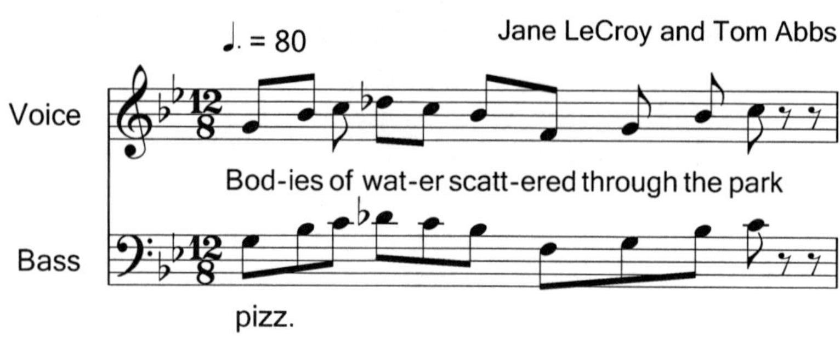

5
Voice
branch-es reach up and scrape the breeze the
Bs.

6
Voice
roots reach down and use cap-ill - ar - y
Bs.

7
Voice
Act-tion in the ci - ty Act-ion in the ci - ty
Bs.

8
Voice
Act-ion in the ci - ty Act-tion in the ci - ty I
Bs.

9
Voice
Bs.
don't want to ca - rry i-

10
Voice
Bs.
3
den-ti - fi - ca - tion a - ny more I

11
Voice
Bs.
don't want to prove I was

12
Voice
Bs.
3
born in nine-teen-sev-en-ty three I

13
Voice
don't
want to be-long to a
Bs.
14
Voice
coun - try
a - ny more
Bs.
15
Voice
don't
want to ca - rry
Bs.
16
Voice
pho - to
i - i - dee
Bs.
17
Bs.

18
Bs.
19
Bs.
20
Bs.
21
Voice
Bod-ies of wat - er have edg-es
Bs.
22
Voice
Lakes and streams and what's in - be-tween
Bs.
23
Voice
Fi-elds and plains and mo oun-tain rang - es
Bs.

24
Voice
High-lands andlow-lands and bad-lands have
Bs.

25
Voice
edg-es have edg-es have
Bs.
4
4

26
Voice
edg-es have edg-es And our
Bs.
4
4

27
Voice
3
hands try to make mo - ore We draw
Bs.

28
Voice
lines on the plan - et with law I
Bs.

29
Voice
don't want to o - be - ey a - ny
Bs.

30
Voice
mo - o - o - re I
Bs.

31
Voice
don't want to o - be - ey a - ny
Bs.

32
Voice
mo - o - o - re
Bs.
33
Repeat ad lib. al fine
Voice
Bs.
34
Fine
Voice
Bs.

## NEEDLE WORKER

I'm back in my old skin
I used to let everyone in

Now I stitch and sew all my holes closed
Put needle and thread to flesh
Gonna fix the rips that have been torn
And bleed myself to Hell

Boys would come and open my doors
I always said "Hello"
Now I take my mouth and stitch it tight
I won't say a word no more

My ears are stitched
My nose is shut
My pores won't sweat at all
My eyes won't see
And my teeth won't bite
I'm a closed woman

My heart's been taken apart by men
Never gonna let that happen again
Gonna close the window between my legs
Please no one but myself

I was a wild woman tamed by a boy
My volatile self turned calm
It was my own mistake, I'm a hurricane
My life with the boy was the eye of the storm

Now the wind slides over and tears it all down
I'm twining, weaving, braiding, looming
I'm a needle worker woman
Sewing my own

I'm back in my old skin

## SHOE REPAIR

At the shoe repair, the man fixes shoes
a woman walks in and says, *I got the blues*
*Can you fix my soul?*

The man said *no* but he took her home
his apartment was small but it's better than alone
they stayed up all night playing each other's bones
bones bones bones

Morning came, man said, *Time to go*
Woman said, *Wait, I want you to know*
*the wind blows through my chest*
*like I haven't any skin*
*the worst part is I'm missing my heart*
*I forget who I left it in*

The man replied, *Didn't you know,*
*we're only skeletons, we're only skeletons*
*Did you think that it would be different? I'm sorry*

At the shoe repair the man fixes shoes
a boy walks in and says, *I got bad news*
*I think my tongue is broke*
*everytime I speak, I choke*
*I can't say what I mean*
*and when I try, I start to scream!*

Then a man came in to complain
his stitching was loose and his eyeholes were lame
a line formed around the block
people trying to get into the shoe repair shop

The shoe repair man said,
*I haven't any tools*
*to fix your broken walks, walking*
*pails and pails of leather and nails*
*aren't enough to cure all your ails*

The man replied, *Didn't you know,*
*we're only skeletons, we're only skeletons*
*Did you think that it would be different? I'm sorry*

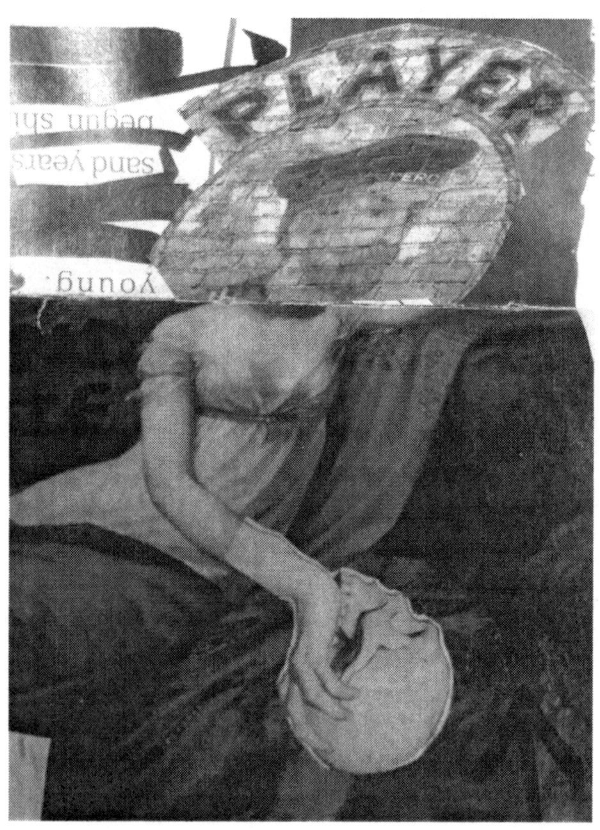

## ALICE SAVINO

I didn't actually say what I wanted to say
before over there, I've been alone all day
and people seem far away

I gave you my hands, my most articulate limbs
If you were a bird would you perch on me?

What goes and comes back?
There are not enough seasons
not enough yo-yos,
not enough cards from card tricks
there are not enough boomerangs
or dogs and fetching sticks
there are not enough things that go and come back

Your words parachuting to my gravity
landing on you rescues me

We all do things we leave
even ourselves leave ourselves
When does one of me change into another of me?
Then who am I to me now,
and who are you when you are gone?

There are not enough things that go and come back
like the moon with its phases,
library books,
migrating birds and loaded fish hooks
and Alice Savino, I wish you were one of those
and could come back to me
like the salty wide tides of the sea

*Note: Alice Savino is Jane LeCroy's grandmother 1922–1993*

# Alice Savino

Jane LeCroy and Tom Abbs

**Slowly - Quasi Recitative ( ♩ = 60)**

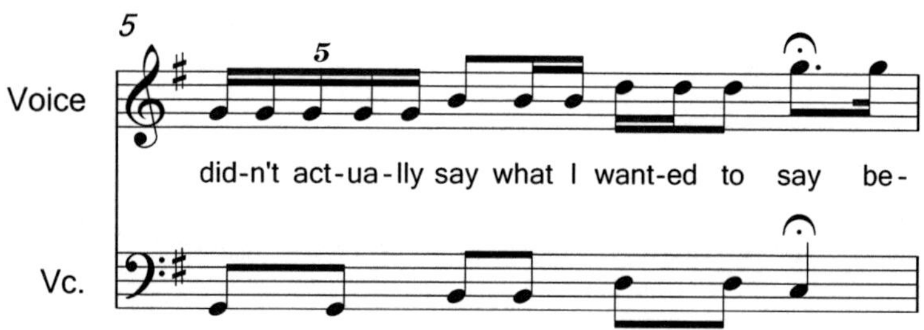


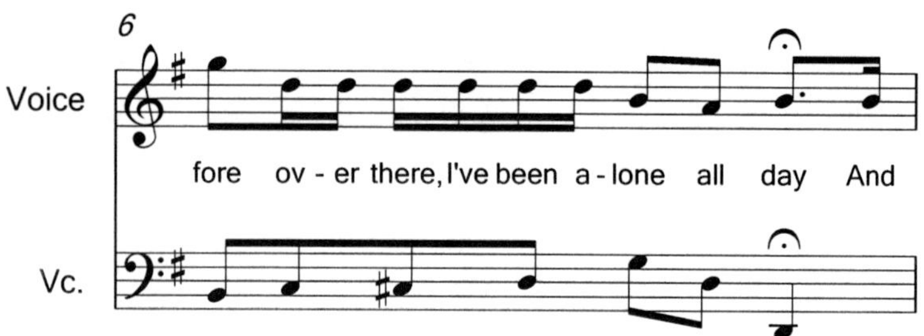

7
Voice
peo-ple seem far a-way peo-ple seem far a-way
Vc.

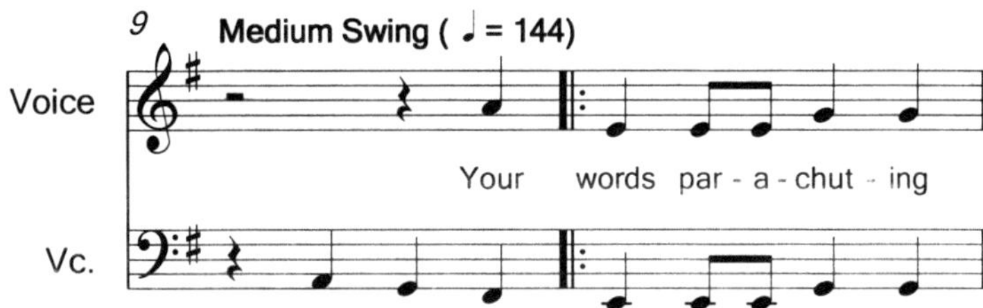
9
Medium Swing ( ♩ = 144)
Voice
Your words par - a - chut - ing
Vc.

11
Voice
to my grav it - y land-ing on you land-ing on you
Vc.

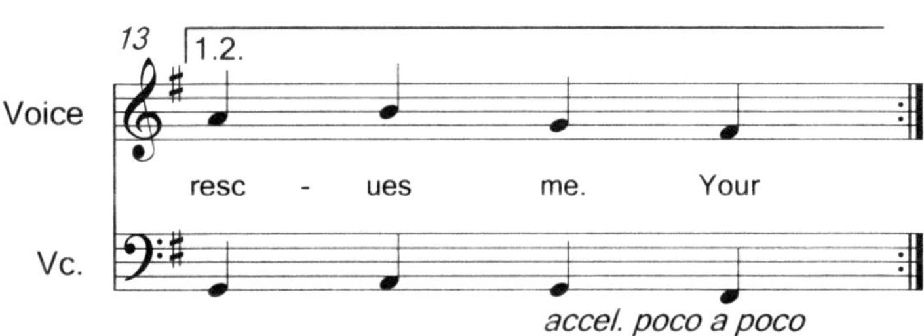
13
1.2.
Voice
resc - ues me. Your
Vc.
accel. poco a poco

## THUNDERBOLT

Old abandoned roller coaster
curled against the sky
blackened by time
rips the wind passing by
squealing ghost riders cling to it
shy

and I say,
        *Are you gonna keep me this time?*
and you say,
        *No*

So, I walk a million miles
underground from train to train
everywhere I go looks the same
never change
I see mad dogs in my room
they aren't really there
they hunger for the moon
as they breathe the steamy air
I set them free in the streets
to roam and howl like grooms
they wander and whine
they don't really care
I want them to save my soul

and I say,
        *Are you gonna keep me this time?*
and you say,
        *No*

*SAVE MY SOUL*
The roller coaster rolls no more

I'm always alone
no one touches me
only the shadows of my memory
what I imagine becomes reality
I let it go and it never comes back to me
you have a pretty mouth and you use it well
every time you speak you send a piece of me to Hell
dogs show up to take me but they never bring me back
I've been waiting to be saved here by the roller coaster track

I keep trying to leave but packs of dogs keep coming
been waiting for the train but the train is not running
the dogs are scarin', howlin', growlin'

Maybe someday the train will come

## RHINOCEROS

9 is divine

The moon is being eaten
by the shadow of the Earth
the moon is made of
rhinoceros skin
it doesn't let anyone in

That's how you are, my darling

I keep taking
bites out of you
but I never get through
I don't care who it is I love
I just want true love

Don't want to break no more
but I keep breaking
losing my pieces
they cover the floor
everywhere you walk
you're walking on me

The rhinoceros
has its horn
the moon is the spike
curled in the sky
it is seeping in my eye

That's how you are, my darling

You haven't been spotted in the wild for years
been throwing my lasso far and near
are you extinct, except in captivity?
orbiting captured by gravity

Come down from the sky
I want to know why
you don't love me
why does nobody love me?
nobody loves me

The rhinoceros tells a story
covered with mud, I add my blood
I want you to be my darling

The moon, the moon, has skin can't get in
this is my darling

## A STORY WITH ICEBERGS

Eventually we must enter the sea
and take our chances with the beasts.

Icebergs are floating white rafts on the sea
seals jump off and swim gracefully
but on the land they move awkwardly;
though there they're safe from the killer whales' deeds
on the land men are predators with their greed.

There's many a story of a magical fish
who grants some wishes to escape the dish;
seals wouldn't fall for it, they have everything they want
but people are filled with longing
and their desires do haunt them.

Once there was a fish
who was caught by one of us,
its silver body plucked from the darkness;
it shone against the white snow and sky
but instead of escaping this was its reply:
Keep me my darling; don't throw me back in the water.

The one holding the net
heard the sad strange plea
and was struck at once by the familiarity
he opened his heart and he embraced the grief;
he envied the seals and jumped into the sea.

# A Story With Icebergs

Jane LeCroy and Tom Abbs

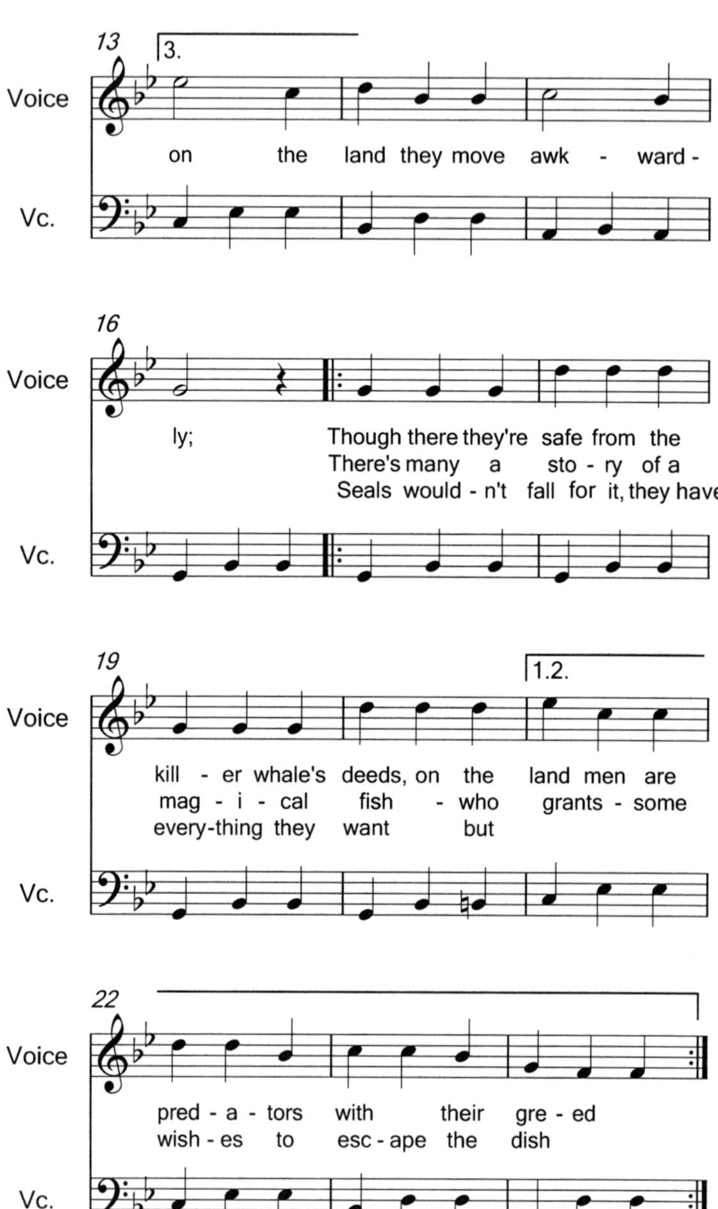
13
3.
Voice
on the land they move awk - ward -
Vc.
16
Voice
ly; Though there they're safe from the
There's many a sto - ry of a
Seals would - n't fall for it, they have
Vc.
19
1.2.
Voice
kill - er whale's deeds, on the land men are
mag - i - cal fish - who grants - some
every-thing they want but
Vc.
22
Voice
pred - a - tors with their gre - ed
wish - es to esc - ape the dish
Vc.

25
3.
Voice
(6.) peo - ple are fi - illed with long - ing
Vc.

28
Voice
and their de - si - res do - o
Vc.

31
1.
2.
Voice
haunt them. Oh, yes Haunt them,
Vc.

34
Voice
haunt them, haunt them!
Vamp
Vc.

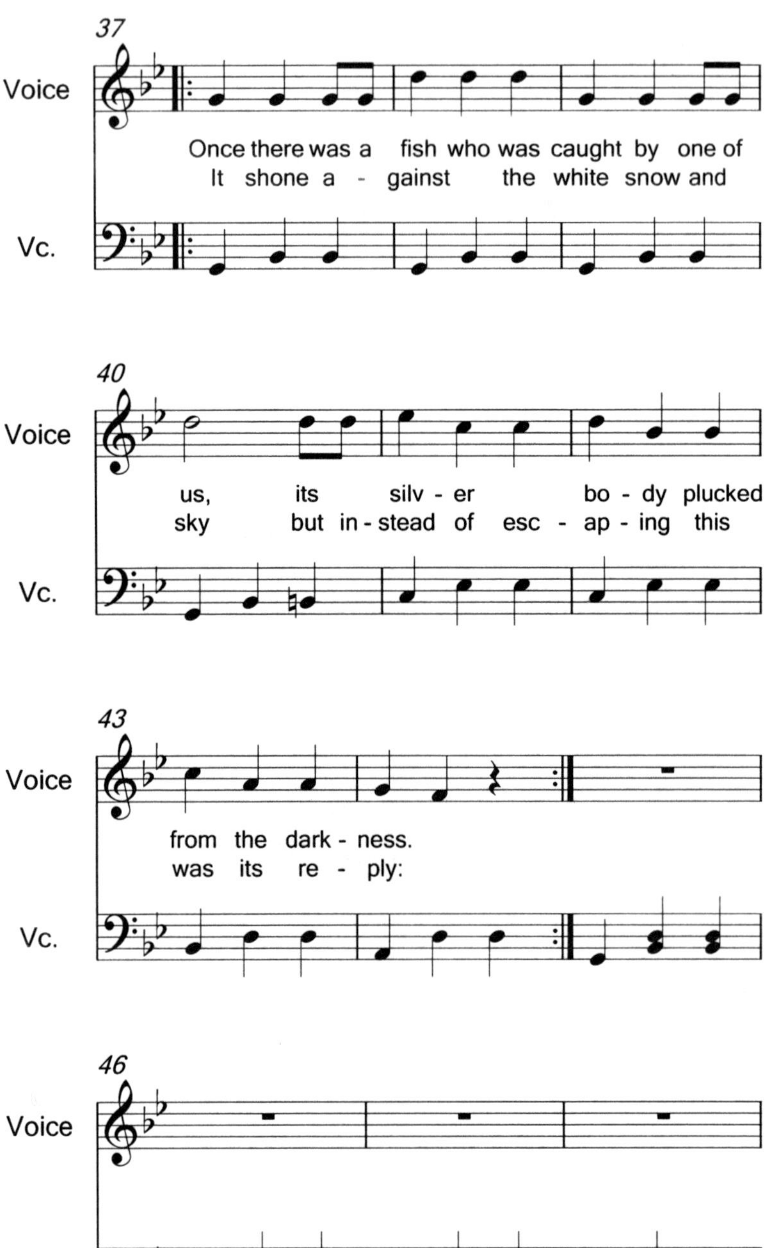
37
Voice
Once there was a fish who was caught by one of
It shone a - gainst the white snow and
Vc.
40
Voice
us, its silv - er bo - dy plucked
sky but in - stead of esc - ap - ing this
Vc.
43
Voice
from the dark - ness.
was its re - ply:
Vc.
46
Voice
Vc.

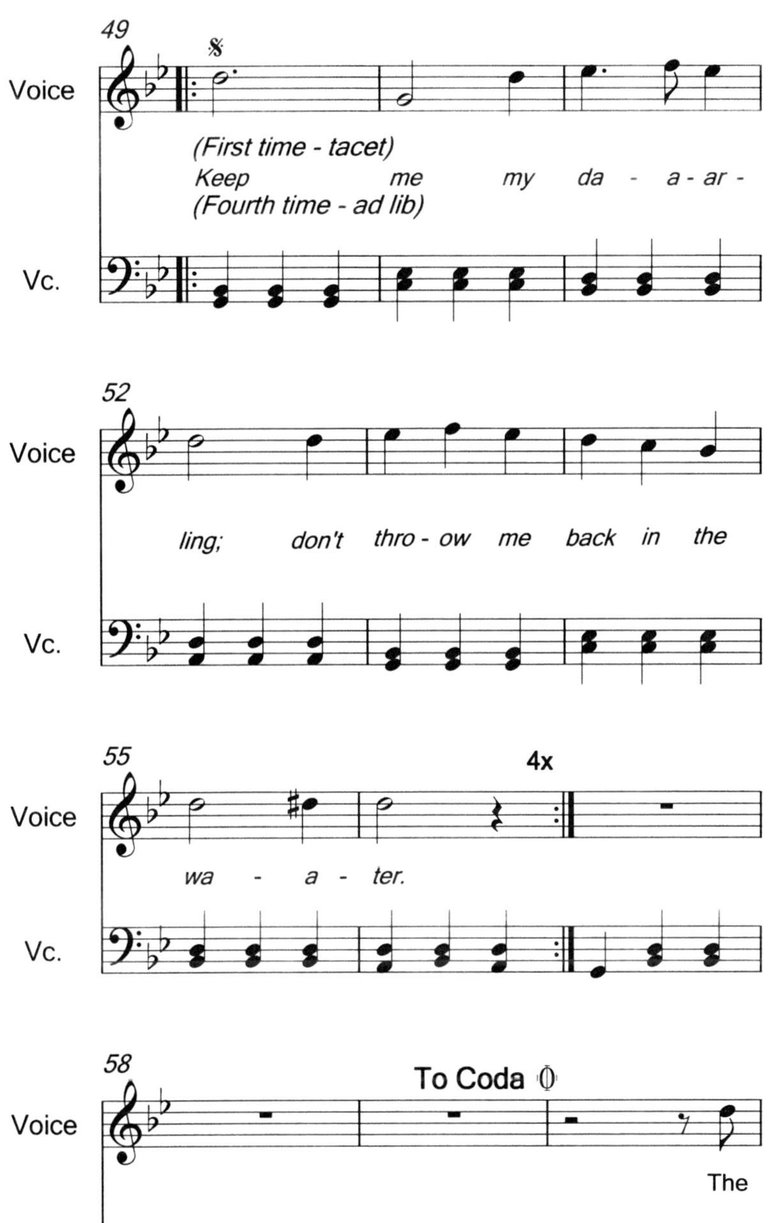
49
Voice
(First time - tacet)
Keep me my da - a - ar -
(Fourth time - ad lib)
Vc.
52
Voice
ling; don't thro - ow me back in the
Vc.
55
4x
Voice
wa - a - ter.
Vc.
58
To Coda
Voice
The
Vc.

61
Voice
one hold-ing the net heard the sad strange
Vc.
64
Voice
plea and was struck at once by the fam-ili-
Vc.
67
Voice
ar - i - ty He op-ened his
Vc.
70
Voice
heart and he em braced the grie -
Vc.

73
Voice
- ef, he
Vc.

76
Voice
env - ied the seals and jumped in - to the
Vc.

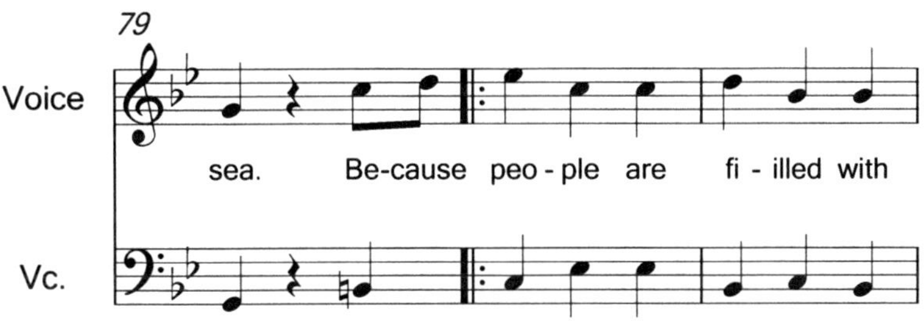
79
Voice
sea. Be-cause peo - ple are fi - illed with
Vc.

82
Voice
long - ing and their des - ir - es
Vc.

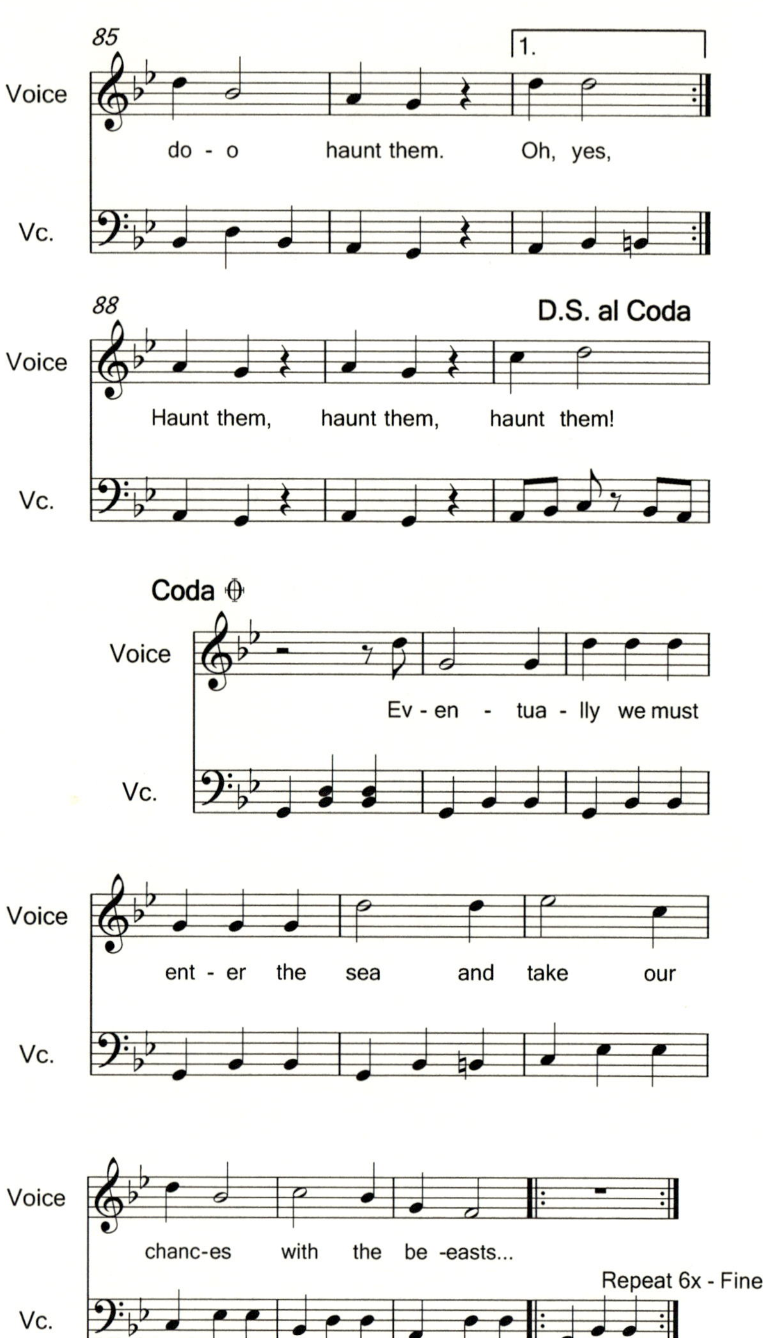
85
1.
Voice
do - o haunt them. Oh, yes,
Vc.
88
D.S. al Coda
Voice
Haunt them, haunt them, haunt them!
Vc.
Coda
Voice
Ev - en - tua - lly we must
Vc.
Voice
ent - er the sea and take our
Vc.
Voice
chanc-es with the be -easts...
Repeat 6x - Fine
Vc.

## BIG BLACK HABIT

My big black habit, the train ride home at 2 a.m.
    the drunk ticket taker.
My luck getting me everywhere, trying to touch everywhere,
    going everywhere but end up nowhere.
Not here, never where I am is where I am, I'm never where I am
    anywhere you see me, I'm gone gone gone.

Seen worse times than this, now I'm just stretching myself thin
    thinner than I've ever been, I'm reaching.
Sick ghost doing cartwheels into the mist
    nodding my head at things I don't understand.
I can't even hear anymore but I don't bother asking, *WHAT?*—
    a smile, a laugh, shrugged you off, your boring story.

Kick back, kicked back,
I'm hard,
no sleep,
insomnia sucking my dreams up
I'm dream dry,
hallucinating
    all the way home on the train
Got to get my dreams somehow

Empty bottle banging up and down the aisle on the train
    spilled coffee, spilled beer on the floor.
    spilled puke from a boy in a baseball cap—
    who's going to clean this mess? I ask you.
Who's going to clean this mess?
Stinking humans, our garbage everywhere, contaminating everything.
    We live in our own shit and call it convenience.

Technology creeps in to replace our telepathy
    our machines are erasing our minds.

We sell our brains for shit boxes to live in,
    a few vacation days we're supposed to be thankful for,
    after giving the best hours of everyday to someone else
    whose getting rich off our sweat
    and I just want to fuck and love and make it home in time.

Not wait on another
concrete
platform
for another late train.
Knowing a million
phones are ringing;
people are so damn lonesome.

The train barrels in and I'm on it holding on,
    all I see is lights on brick buildings all the way back.
I gave up the stars for this?
    I bleached my own sky, its true face erased with my electricity
                tearing holes in me.

## WONDERELLA MARVELLA

Wonderella Marvella
is a beauty queen, is a wet dream
she ought to be an ice cream flavor
want to do her
a favor

She's got lots of sharp things
she's got lots of thin wings
like a bumble bee, like a fairy
like a dragon fly, like a goodbye
like a lie

Wonderella Marvella
elevated and elated
always trying to fly, always getting high
always on the sly, always slipping by
on her way to die

and the world is what it is

When the lights are low and no one's there to see
are you who you are or do you look for who to be?

Are you a victim or a victor?
Are you a player or played for?
Are you on your way there or are you on your way back?
Did you find what you were looking for, you lose what you lacked?
Did you make up your own rules or did you obey theirs?
Do you judge others, do you judge yourself?

Pick your truth, pick your lie
pick your planet, pick your God
pick your poison, pick your pleasure
pick your pain, pick your leisure
It's never what it seems to be but it's always what it is
we wait on line forever
and we forget that we can leave

Wonderella Marvella
is a beauty queen, is a wet dream
she ought to be an ice cream flavor
no one can ever save her
because she is saved
She is saved

*Scan the above QR code to access*
*the musical rendition of this piece*
*performed by*
*Jane LeCroy (vocals) and Tom Abbs (acoustic bass).*

## LINER NOTES

I made up my first song when I was born. It was the same song you sang at your birth. You made it up too. I was put in a crib with a velvet painting of Jimi Hendrix above it. My ears were fed lots of Hendrix, Led Zepplin and Pink Floyd from my father and lots of Tom Waits, Leonard Cohen and Captain Beefheart from my mother, and lots of Harry Nilsson and Joni Mitchell from the decade I was born into.

I made up my first song when I was three years old and would curl up on the big pillow in the bass kick drum while my dad's rock band rehearsed. I would put my fingers in my ears and sing my own words along with whatever song the band played. My beloved grandmother, Alice Savino, a very literary woman from the 1920s, shared with me from birth: poems, rhymes and prayers she knew by heart. I learned them by heart too and continue to love learning things by heart. I have been making poetry since I learned how to talk.

I made up my first song when I was about six years old. I would drag my cousin Arlene into my Uncle Dan's room in the basement of my grandparent's house and just start improvising melody and lyrics for minutes at a time. I would tell her I had made up the songs beforehand just because I thought that would be more impressive to her, but really the songs were composed on the spot. I would demand Arlene make up songs for me.

I made up my first song when I was in Middle School, around twelve years old. I had this enormous walk between my school and home, along the way I would make up songs. I never sang them for anyone. I rarely remembered them to really work on, but I was always crafting and expounding to the beat of my walk and the incessant rush of thruway traffic that was the background of my life growing up in Nyack, New York. As I approached teendom, Rap was born. I tuned in my boom-box in the middle of the night to hear the new music; I'd get the radio signals from the nearby Bronx, I was seduced by Rap and Hip Hop. As I wandered the radio waves I also found college stations that turned me on to Punk Rock and New Wave. I love music. All along I wrote lots and lots of poetry, the music of language.

I made up my first song out of heartbreak when I was twenty years old, breaking up with the first lover I had ever lived with. It was "Needle Worker" and I sang it to my good friends Melissa York and Raphael (Heatley) LaMotta, who comprised the emocore-punk band, Vitapup with Greg Griffith. They were so enthusiastic about my raw singing I was invited to perform with them at the raucous rock/punk dive bar, Continental, on Third Ave. and St. Marks Place in the East Village. I performed a capella in the middle of Vitapup's set. To our shock, the audience became silent as I belted out my song. It was so well received, I didn't stop singing and have done what I could to be up on the stage ever since. I continued to perform Spoken Word and a capella singing with Vitapup, solo, during their set. We toured. We made a record, *An Hour With Vitapup* (1995) that featured "Build Your Own Home." We played and played. Producer, Hi-Fi Hillary Johnson approached me and encouraged me to start recording myself, she set-me up in her studio and we produced, *Lickety-Split*, a solo a capella cassette that had a playing card as the insert, it was 1994.

I first saw Tom Abbs play when I was in college with him at The New School in New York City in the early 90s. I was at Lang studying poetry with Christian McEwen, Sekou Sundiata and Kurt Lamkin, who taught me the performance poem/live poem. Tom Abbs attended the Jazz school and had a regular gig at a bar on First Ave. and 1st Street in the East Village. I would listen to him play upright jazz bass every week, improvisation. I fell in love with jazz. It was my dream to play with Tom Abbs.

I never had the nerve to ask any musicians to play with me because I considered myself a poet and didn't feel enough of a musician to invite musicians to collaborate with me; though many jazz musicians invited me to perform my improvised Spoken Word with them, including: Reggie Workman, Andy Bemkey and Erik Lawrence. Around this same time I was performing lots of my poetry and Spoken Word at the Nuyorican, Cornelia St. Cafe and avant-garde performance art spaces like the Gargoyle Mechanique and the Collective Unconscious. I was published in

Fast Folk Magazine a few times and was invited by Jack Hardy to be part of his songwriters group that met every week in his apartment in The Village. There, I listened to songwriters work out their songs, I performed my poetry. Though I wasn't singing yet, I was embraced and nurtured by these communities of musicians.

It was at Jack Hardy's that I met singer songwriter Carol Lipnik, who entirely inspired me and made me want to sing my poems. We became close friends and she was the first person I sang to seriously, in the back of a car parked outside of a venue she played at. It was because of her I started singing publicly, and shared my new endeavor with my friends in Vitapup. Carol Lipnik only encouraged me, and we sometimes write together. In this collection she collaborated with me in the creation of the songs, "Eldorado" and "Last Dance," she has also honored me by interpreting and performing "Traveling." Both "Traveling" and "Last Dance" appear on her record *Cloud Girl* (2005) on Mermaid Alley Music.

After my solo performances with Vitapup started happening, where I was singing my poetry in addition to performing Spoken Word, some rock musicians, including Scott Garapolo, Alessanda Bocco and Dean Haggerty, wanted to collaborate with me; the band Spook Engine was formed and we put out *Sounds of an Approaching Era* (1996) on Bloodlink Records, the same label that put out my 7-inch vinyl Spoken Word single, *Guilty* (1995). One time, Spook Engine had a much anticipated show planned at the Knitting Factory; a week prior to the show, band members had some personal issues that prevented them from being able to perform and I found myself without a band. Desperate, and with a prestigious venue date, I finally had the nerve to ask my favorite jazz bassist, Tom Abbs, if he would accompany me.

We had one rehearsal where I sang him a few of my songs. Back then he played upright bass with a didgeridoo tied to it and percussion toys tied to his shoes—even firecrackers tied to his bass bridge! We played the show as a duo, our work together had an ease of communication so that it was as if we were just transmitting the poetry and music; having had only one rehearsal, and both being improvisational artists, half our set was improvised. The crowd loved it and so did we. We started making records and playing shows all over the country. We held a weekly residency at The Internet Café on 3rd Street between First and Second Ave. from 1999 to 2001, we invited guest poets and musicians to join us every week, always keeping our set half improvised, taking ideas from the audience to weave our art. We had a monthly residency at Bowery Poetry Club on Bowery from 2003 to 2007 and another residency at the Liberty Science Center in 2007. Starting in 2012 we have a monthly residency at Goodbye Blue Monday in Bushwick, Brooklyn. This book is a collection of some of the signature lyric poems Tom Abbs and I set to music in our collaboration we call TRANSMITTING that began in 1998. We are transmitting the poetry and music, we are conduits together. Thank you for receiving us.

Special thanks to everyone mentioned here and: Kevin A. Virgilio, who transcribed the songs for print; Booklyn Artists Alliance, which has supported my work and published my poetry; and David Last who developed and performed some of these songs with me in our electronica band, Somnaut; and Kid Lucky and his hip hop, a capella orchestra, Nu Voices; and to Bradford Reed who produced our record *From the Inside* (2003) featuring the recording available in this book: "Moonscape;" and to Geoff Mann who produced our record *Dark and Full of Life* (2007) on Delphy Records, featuring the recordings available in this book: "Lost My Way," "Mosquito," "Wonderella Marvella" and "Flying Piece;" and to Renee Silverman for creating the video for "Mosquito"; and Alyse Milomir Raðenović for creating many videos including ones for: "Wonderella Marvella" and "Flying Piece" and to Three Rooms Press: Kat Georges and Peter Carlaftes, because of whom, this book exists.

## ABOUT THE AUTHOR

JANE LECROY is a New York based poet, singer and performance artist, home-birthing mother of three, teacher, atheist, vegetarian, televisionless, hedonist who has collaborated, performed and toured with: the SF-based all-women poetry troupe, Sister Spit; the 1990s emo-core band, Vitapup; the electronica project, Somnaut; the a capella hip-hop beatboxing orchestra, Nu Voices; and Brant Lyon's Hydrogen Jukebox. She fronts the avant-pop band Transmitting, featuring multi-instrumentalists Tom Abbs and David Rogers-Berry. Jane teaches and publishes student work through the artist-in-the-schools organizations Teachers & Writers Collaborative and Dreamyard. Jane's previous book of poetry, *Names*, was published by Booklyn as part of the award-winning ABC chapbook series, the latest Transmitting record is *Dark and Full of Life* on the European label, Delphy Entertainment Rekords.

## ABOUT THE COMPOSER

TOM ABBS studied jazz performance and composition at the New School in the early 90s where he met Jane while she was at Lang a few blocks away. He spent much of the 90s playing bass around NYC and doing artist residencies in the public schools. In 1998 he founded the not-for-profit Jump Arts, which presented musicians, poets, painters and dancers in performance spaces around New York and the eastern seaboard. He later went on to be the General Manager of the legendary Rock and Jazz label ESP-Disk and is now co-owner and CEO of the record label Northern Spy. Tom has played on over 40 albums on bass, tuba, cello and other assorted instruments and is a current member of the Hungry March Band and Transmitting, with Jane LeCroy and David Rogers-Berry.

# books on three rooms press

## POETRY

Hala Alyan
*Atrium*

Peter Carlaftes
*DrunkYard Dog*
*I Fold with the Hand I Was Dealt*

Joie Cook
*When Night Salutes the Dawn*

Thomas Fucaloro
*Inheriting Craziness is Like a Soft Halo of Light*

Patrizia Gattaceca
*Isula d'Anima / Soul Island*

Kat Georges
*Our Lady of the Hunger*
*Punk Rock Journal*

Robert Gibbons
*Close to the Tree*

Karen Hildebrand
*One Foot Out the Door*
*Take a Shot at Love*

Matthew Hupert
*Ism is a Retrovirus*

David Lawton
*Sharp Blue Stream*

Jane LeCroy
*Signature Play*

Dominique Lowell
*Sit Yr Ass Down or You Ain't gettin no Burger King*

Jane Ormerod
*Recreational Vehicles on Fire*
*Welcome to the Museum of Cattle*

Jackie Sheeler
*to[o] long*

Angelo Verga
*Praise for What Remains*

George Wallace
*Poppin' Johnny*
*EOS: Abductor of Men*

## PHOTOGRAPHY-MEMOIR

Mike Watt
*On & Off Bass*

## FICTION

Michael T. Fournier
*Hidden Wheel*

Richard Vetere
*The Writers Afterlife*

## DADA

*Maintenant: Journal of Contemporary Dada Art & Literature*
(Annual poetry/art journal, since 2003)

## SHORT STORIES

*Have a NYC: New York Short Stories*
Annual Short Fiction Anthology

## HUMOR

Peter Carlaftes
*A Year on Facebook*

## PLAYS

Madeline Artenberg &
Karen Hildebrand
*The Old In-and-Out*

Peter Carlaftes
*Triumph For Rent (3 Plays)*
*Teatrophy (3 More Plays)*

Larry Myers
*Mary Anderson's Encore*
*Twitter Theater*

## TRANSLATIONS

Patrizia Gattaceca
*Isula d'Anima / Soul Island*
(poems in Corsican with English translations)

George Wallace
*EOS: Abductor of Men* (American poems with Greek translations)

three rooms press | new york, ny
current catalog: www.threeroomspress.com

CPSIA information can be obtained at www.ICGtesting.com
Printed in the USA
LVOW13s1937031113

359783LV00003B/85/P